THE
PHYSICAL SIDE
OF
LEARNING

A
Parent-Teacher's
Guidebook
of
Physical Activities Kids Need
To Be Successful In School

by
Dr. Leela C. Zion

EDITOR
Frank Alexander

COVER DESIGN
Frank Alexander & Laura Zerzan

TEXT ILLUSTRATIONS
Laura Zerzan

Published by:
Front Row Experience,
540 Discovery Bay Blvd., Byron, CA 94514-9454

i

NOTICE
The information
contained in this book
is true and complete
to the best of our knowledge.
It is offered with no guarantees
on the part of the author or Front Row Experience.
The author and publisher disclaim all liability
in connection with the use of this book.

Published
by
FRONT ROW EXPERIENCE
540 Discovery Bay Blvd.
Byron, CA 94514-9454

To the memory of my brother,
Harry Edwin Bryan,
whose love and encouragement
are eternal.

ACKNOWLEDGMENTS

Many people have contributed to the work that led to the writing of this book. I owe a large debt to those who have been my teachers through the years: Jane Shurmer, Valerie Hunt, Newell Kephart, T. Bentley Edwards, and Ray Barsch.

I am grateful to my colleagues and friends who have been directly helpful in this project: Kathryn Corbett, Jan Menninga, Betty Lou Raker, Lynn Warner, and Louise Watson.

I would like to extend my thanks to my excellent illustrator, Laura Zerzan and my knowledgeable and helpful publisher, Frank Alexander.

I am especially indebted to my editor, Patsy Givins, whose gentle coaching will some day turn me into a writer.

ABOUT THE AUTHOR

Dr. Leela C. Zion is eminently qualified to advise parents and teachers in child development. She has taught first and fourth grades, high school, and university levels for the past 40 years. She was the senior author with Betty Lou Raker of **THE PHYSICAL SIDE OF THINKING**, published by Charles C. Thomas, 1986. **THE PHYSICAL SIDE OF LEARNING** parallels this book and simplifies many of the concepts presented. Dr. Zion has taught perceptual-motor development and elementary school physical education courses at Humbolt State University, Humboldt, California, for the last 34 years. She has directed graduate research in many areas including perceptual-motor development. After obtaining her Master's degree in Education at Stanford University, Dr. Zion worked on her doctoral dissertation entitled: "Body Concept As It Relates To Self Concept", and obtained her Doctorate in Education at the University of California, Berkeley, in 1963. In the early 1970's she began formal studies in perceptual-motor development, studying under such luminaries as Newell Kephart, Ray Barsch and Bryant Cratty. She has worked continually over the years with elementary school and special education teachers in developing perceptual-motor programs in their schools. She is presently working on a book on body concept designed to clarify the complications of our culture in developing self esteem.

CONTENTS

Chapter 3
SPATIAL AND TEMPORAL AWARENESS -------- 25

Chapter 4
DIRECTIONALITY --- 32

Chapter 9
WHAT NEXT? -- 79

BIBLIOGRAPHY -- 82

INTRODUCTION

We do not come equipped with bodies that know up from down or right from left, or ears that respond to English, nor do we come with the capacity to run or read. These are learned through many years of experience and practice. Learning is the most wonderful game in life, especially when we can learn easily and safely. The more carefully selected the experiences and practices, the more efficient and rapid will be the learning.

Some children will learn many of the activities in this book through the course of their development. Unfortunately, they are in the minority. Today, our high school graduates are reading, on average, at the fourth grade reading level. And most of these poor readers have been through numerous remedial reading programs by the time they graduate. Most of these poor readers did not start out reading with all the physical capacities needed to be efficient learners. It is those physical capacities that will be developed in this book.

If we can get our children started early with the physical perceptions necessary for reading, writing and math, they will succeed in school and happily pursue the wonders of learning. When children start late and are always behind and trying to catch up, their self-esteem will be in jeopardy. The intellectual capacities of children do not level out at some miraculous age, regardless of their experiences or lack of experiences.

This book is based on the most current information available on perceptual-motor development, on my own exploration and research, and the latest philosophical developments in the mind/body relationship. The works of Jean Piaget and Patricia Smith Churchland have contributed significantly to my understanding of learning, as will be clearly seen in my application of their works.

Knowledge develops from action. All new events are experienced by their physical realities. More advanced understanding originates in action and develops through actions. Movement is essential to the functioning of all our senses and to the structuring and unifying of information.

This book is not designed to create geniuses. Rather, I hope to help adults help youngsters develop the basic perceptual-motor patterns that underlie the advanced capacities involved in learning. Neither is this book designed to create athletes, although that might seem a logical result from this program. (Most athletes have very specialized abilities in addition to general perceptual-motor abilities.) Nor is this book designed to produce physical fitness, though certainly some degrees of fitness will result. This book is designed to help relatively normal children prepare for school, although it should be even more helpful for the development of children with physical or learning impairments.

Parents and teachers want children to succeed in school. There is much evidence indicating the close relationships between perception, movement and learning efficiency. These relationships will be explained so that the reader may understand how learning takes place, especially in regard to reading, writing and math.

The activities at the end of each chapter deal with teaching and playing with children in ways that will provide the basic body awareness, spatial and temporal awareness, balance, directionality, body concept, and mastery needed to help children with the physical patterns necessary to learn in school. Many children enter school ill-prepared for learning because their bodies haven't been well prepared to help them learn. Developing these capacities will not necessarily be a panacea that solves all the ills of all the children, but for most children, and especially children who are hyperactive, dyslexic, or having difficulty succeeding in school, this program will be helpful.

This book is designed to get parents and children started on a successful pattern of mutual learning and accomplishment in play. Minimal equipment will be needed: two balls, two beanbags, a mat or thick rug, two large sheets of paper and crayons, some furniture, a 2 x 4 board, and some indoor or outdoor space.

Chapters 2 through 7 deal with the specific learning processes necessary for learning: body awareness, spatial/temporal awareness, directionality, balance, body concept and self-esteem, and mastery. Chapter 8 integrates all these components into a comprehensive whole, while providing explanations for the relational basis of sensation, movement and learning. Chapter 9 provides ideas for future development.

The use of the words he or she or he/she or s/he have not been solved to my satisfaction, so I will use he in one chapter and she in the next.

Chapter 1

LEARNING AND TEACHING, BRIEFLY

Our cultural system is changing and more parents are working. Most parents do not have college degrees in teaching. Most parents are not even trained in parenting, the most important thing we do on this planet. So, how do I get you to find time and knowledge sufficient to succeed in helping your child to learn how to learn? If the time spent with your child is enjoyable and profitable, then I believe you will become motivated. And the more involved you become in this program, the more motivated you will be. I believe parent-child interaction is extremely important and most parents can learn to deal comfortably and profitably with their children through constructive play.

Parents are the first teachers and their job is to empower children.

LEARNING

Learning is a change in behavior that is relatively permanent. Learning and memory are very closely related.

Learning cannot result from electrical or chemical stimulation. We can change behavior through such stimulation, making one more aggressive, calm, nervous or amorous, but these methods cannot supply the basic sensory input necessary for permanent learning. In order to produce meaning that is retained by the learner, sensory information must be related to meaningful activities. We learn by experimenting with our environment almost as a scientist learns in a laboratory. When an infant manipulates a blanket with her hand, she watches her hand and relates what she sees as the movement of the blanket to what is being felt in the manipulating process. She learns that a plastic block or a teddy bear each change shape as they are rotated. She also recognizes that this is not a visual distortion but is the same object seen from different viewpoints.

AIDS TO LEARNING

Learning is easiest if all sensory systems are concentrating on the same item of information at the same time. As the infant holds and manipulates a banana with her hands, she will learn more if she is also looking at the banana instead of looking at an apple, tasting and smelling the banana instead of an apple, hearing the word banana instead of the word apple. Concentrated attention helps make learning more efficient.

Positive reinforcement also aids in effective learning. Being rewarded lets the child know that what she is doing is good. She also knows that she is doing it well, or at least better than she did it before. Knowledge of results can be a reward in itself.

Motivation is another important element in learning. If your child knows why you want her to do something and how it will apply in her life, and she values these purposes, she will be much more enthusiastic about accomplishing such tasks.

Learning is developed through various encounters with the environment where one learns to interpret incoming information with more and more precision. With practice the individual will learn to develop many possible responses, and the most appropriate one will be available and employed for even slight changes in circumstances.

Through such learning experiences, the child begins to develop strategies, involving choices and depending on circumstances. We first learn strategies in the process of trying to get what we need or want from our parents. Later we will learn strategies to help us deal with brothers and sisters, aunts and uncles, grandparents, the bully next door and each different school teacher and boss we encounter in our lifetime.

Parents of children who are slow in some regard are often told "to wait". They are often told "When she's ready to do it, she will." The activities in this book will help your child become ready. Research and clinical experience have clearly indicated that if these physical capacities are well-prepared, youngsters will fit appropriately into the reading, writing, and math programs offered in the primary grades.

TEACHING

The way we teach is based on what we know about how people learn. Teaching is designed to help people learn efficiently and effectively with the most joy possible. Why should it be otherwise?

Remember, your job as teacher/parent is to empower your child.

Starting Out

1) Be sure you have your child's attention when you start by help-ing her learn to focus on the important elements in the environ-ment. Eliminate extraneous noise or visually distracting ele-ments in the environment so that you and she are the stars of the show. You get a child's attention by giving your attention to the child.

2) Show the child the book illustration of the activity you are to be doing.

3) Talk about the elements of the activity and how to go about each one.

4) Discuss the goals of the activity and what meaning it may have for her and her abilities to perform well.

5) Demonstrate the activity for the child. You don't have to be an all-star. Just doing the basic movement pattern as best you can is sufficient.

6) Let the child do the activity. Go slowly at first. Sometimes it is helpful for the child to do the first part of a movement and then the middle part and then the last part.

7) Use positive reinforcement, giving compliments on the good things done, giving a high five or some version of approval and joy.

8) Repeat the activity several times, until the child is comfortable and successful. Kids like to repeat actions.

Be sure the task is understood. Talk through each element, if necessary. Sometimes several demonstrations will be helpful. Use positive reinforcement as often as possible. The objective is to help your child succeed.

Although if may sound boring, endless repetition and practice opportunities are important to the development of automatic, smooth and efficient movements. Repetition can be enjoyable if the child is having a degree of success and is achieving increasing mastery.

Stop your sessions a little before your child wants to stop. One of the best ways to keep motivation high is to leave an activity at a high point, before boredom or fatigue has set in. Don't overdo it no matter how much fun it is.

Every day repeat some of the activities you did on the preceding day and then add new ones. Go fast enough to avoid boredom but not so fast that your child does not master what the lesson offers.

Although you may not know everything there is to know about teaching and learning, the important thing is to begin. Once you have started, then you will have appropriate questions to ask and can look for the answers and change your teaching process. Continue to observe results, ask more questions, find more answers, try new things, on and on, as you get better and better.

PREASSESSMENT

It is difficult even for teachers to assess thoroughly the abilities of their students, but having some idea of the strengths and weaknesses of your child will give you a basis for the selection of activities. When you become familiar with the elements of this program, you can emphasize activities that fit the needs of your child more specifically.

Ask yourself the following questions as you watch your child:

1) Does my child maintain balance easily?

2) Does my child have reasonable body posture?

3) Does my child appear to be comfortable when doing tasks?

4) Does my child have the ability to distinguish right from left?

5) Does my child avoid bumping into objects or other children?

6) Is my child generally accident-free?

7) Does my child have reasonable coordination?

If your child is of kindergarten age or older, add the following questions:

8) Can my child hop on one foot?

9) Can my child gallop or skip?

10) Can my child broad jump?

11) Can my child high jump?

12) Can my child throw a ball with some accuracy?

13) Can my child draw simple forms?

14) Can my child build with blocks?

If your child is of average development, she will be able to do all of these activities to some extent. If she is unable to do some of the activities, note if she falls into one particular category, such as balance or directionality. Then go to the chapter dealing with that capacity and pick activities that will improve her specific difficulty.

The need for children to move appropriately must be viewed in terms of their learning potential. Many abilities will emerge with experience, but to reach their full potential their activities must be purposefully planned. This book is designed to get you started in that planning. Once you and your child get involved and motivated, together you can develop additional activities that will meet your individual needs.

You can determine particular areas of strength you would like to develop in your child and go directly to the chapter covering that topic and progress from there. Or you can proceed one chapter at a time with activities you prefer to work on at first. Chapters are arranged in developmental sequence and will progress to more difficult activities by the end of the book. It will be best if you read the explanatory text before you pick out an activity for your child so that you will have some idea what the activity will accomplish and can explain it.

Encourage your child to create new ways to do things as well as create new activities. At the end of each session praise your child and express your love for her. Bypass an activity if your child reacts negatively to it.

Learning is life's most exciting game.

GENERAL DEVELOPMENT ACTIVITIES

There are many general kinds of activities that parents can provide in addition to the specific activities in this book that will help your children become more aware of their bodies and better prepared for learning. These activities will include much laughter and giggling, especially if you participate with your child. The more fun, the better. They include the following

Swimming
Swimming is especially important, not only because of the unusual interrelationship between gravity and buoyancy, but because of the intensive tactual learning that takes place. Understanding the limits of one's body by increasing the tactual stimulus to the skin is very important in developing body boundaries. Being free of the downward pull of gravity and influenced by the upward push of buoyancy presents new challenges and new interpretations of what the world is all about.

Tumbling
Tumbling activities, from simple rolling on the floor to somersaults and headstands, aid tremendously in the child's development of a sense of balance, directionality and space/time relationships. These activities need not and should not be performed with any thoughts of

Olympic competence. The objective is not ideal form and perfection, but simple experimentation with one's body and with establishing lifelong kinesthetic processes, enabling one to move efficiently.

Running

Running is not only delightful but establishes knowledge about one's capacities. Running around the room, running around the house, running around the yard, running around the block, all help your child to understand how fast and how far she can go. She will understand how much energy it takes and how soon she is apt to get tired. Eventually she will understand that she can outrun Jimmy but not Mary. She will know how much to exert to catch up with someone, or slow down to be caught up to.

It might be helpful for some children if their parents would define a 100 yard area in a parking lot or on a playground or in a field, so the youngster can be timed and begin to understand time in relationship to space. She will also have the opportunity to compare her new times with her old times covering the same distance, if that is desired. Similarly, measurements could be taken of how far your child can broad jump or high jump, or how high a fence or couch your youngster can vault over.

For some youngsters, races will be important. These can be easily arranged with neighborhood kids, or in school settings. Some youngsters are more competitive than others and often need such comparisons for motivation. Many other youngsters are just interested in how well they can do compared to the last time they tried something, comparing their times or distances with last week's or last year's best. Like checking changes in height and weight and tracking these changes, you may wish to track the progress of the child's speed and endurance.

Strength

Learning how strong we are is as important for girls as for boys.

Being able to carry the grocery bag in from the car, move the furniture around, push and pull against other children, or lift weights are all ways of learning what our bodies are capable of.

We all need to learn to be in control of ourselves. Not necessarily all the time, but certainly when we want to be. Some children are hyperactive, with little control, and need to learn relaxation in order to reduce stress and be in control of themselves.

We all need to learn the limits of our bodies or we will find ourselves in excessive pain when we overdo and try to be Herculean in our daily lives. Knowing which parts of our bodies are weak or can be pained easily will help us to achieve more pleasure in life as well as extend our life span.

Health And Heart Rate
You can get your child started on understanding her body and taking responsibility and care of it by teaching her to find her own heart beat. Just have her put her right hand over her heart and listen and feel. When she can hear it, have her count the beat out loud. Using a watch with a second hand tell her when to start counting, time her for a minute and tell her to stop. Experiment with activities that make the heart beat faster and take her pulse rate, then try resting activities and compare results. Have her time your pulse and time your heart rate, too.

Risks
Success and failure make and break us all the time. As we gain confidence in ourselves, we will learn which things we can master and which things we either need to overcome or avoid. Our capacities for risk-taking are related to the successes we have had in life. We all must start out taking tiny risks and succeeding before we can take larger and larger risks.

As we develop our sense of self, we learn how much to trust ourselves and others, and we learn something of cooperation and competition. Some of us are more prone to cooperate, others are more prone to compete. And many of us do both quite comfortably. The more knowledgeable we are about ourselves, the more freedom we have to pick and choose the things that give us pleasure and that develop us into something greater.

Chapter 2

BODY AWARENESS

GENERAL DEVELOPMENT

The developing intellect grows as the child experiments by acting on objects, observing the effects of the action and incorporating new constructions of the world into his being. The child compares the effects of his actions on similar objects and systematizes this learning into generalizations that utilize similarities and differences. The child experiences his body as he experiences his world. He learns where his body ends and the rest of the world begins. He learns how to move his arms and legs and head. He learns how long or short they are or powerful or weak. He learns how to curl his fingers around objects that excite him and carry them to his mouth for further investigation. He cannot function without body awareness.

At first, infants learn simple ways of manipulating objects by pushing, pulling, twisting, dropping, smelling, tasting and looking at them. It is important to provide opportunities for the child to act on objects and see how the objects react and then have the child vary the action and see what a difference it makes. All knowledge is constructed by the individual as he acts on objects and people and tries to make sense out of his experience.

Throughout a person's entire life he will perceive all other physical realities in relation to his own body. The reality of what we call "me" will affect everything we experience.

As the child improves his understanding of his own body, he improves his connection to the environment by way of sensory input and movement interaction. The child continually learns about himself and others, and the more varied experiences a child can have, the greater will be his understanding of himself and his world. It will take some practice to learn how to fit his body through a hole in the fence or duck under a rope or climb into a truck bed.

By the time a child is two, he should have started developing internal constructs from sensory and movement experiences that aid in the efficiency of moving, thinking, learning and reading. These include capacities to deal with gravity, balance, motion, leverage, force, space/time, mass/weight, and inertia/energy. Although these qualities might be more easily studied in a physics lab, they are related to everything we do, whether we move or not, whether we are conscious of it or not. The development of these interrelationships with the environment can evolve haphazardly or in an efficient and well-planned manner.

CONSTRUCTION OF REALITY

As the infant increasingly experiences the environment and increasingly constructs a personal reality, he develops his sense of body awareness. In infancy, and when learning new things, most of the interactions that occur involve conscious thought. As experience broadens, there are unconscious patterns that may be called into operation to execute the actions desired, stored in various areas of the brain. These automatic patterns only develop after many, many repetitions. When your child first learns to walk he must use conscious effort to control what he is doing or he will fall down. With appropriate amounts of practice, patterns will develop that will become unconscious and automatic. They allow the individual to think about other things instead of the movement itself. The child can then think about where he is walking, not how to walk, what he is writing, not how to write, or what he is going to do tomorrow while he rides his bike to the store.

The greater the child's body awareness, the easier it is to develop these automatic patterns. For instance, in order to answer the door bell it is necessary to determine where one is in space/time---sitting, standing, lying down---where in the house one is located, where the front door is, and all the movements one must execute to get from the present position and location to the front door. We do this at unconscious levels and we usually pick the best route of several alternatives before we move. The greater one's body awareness, the more efficient one will be in getting to the front door without tripping on something or bumping into a chair.

Body awareness and awareness of others go hand in hand. As we learn the size and shape and capacities of our bodies, we learn the relationships of ourselves to everything in our external world. A person knows very little about his body unless he moves it. He knows very little about the outside world unless he moves in it.

EMBODIMENT

Body awareness involves embodiment, which is fully experiencing one's body, feeling all sensory input and rejoicing in both input and output. Each of us learns to perceive variations in the state of our bodily being and detect what enhances life and what diminishes it. Each of us learns what works for us in our daily life regarding strength, speed, endurance, flexibility, rest, stress, risk taking, ways of interacting, ways of exercising, ways of reaching trust, comfort and satisfaction. Embodiment involves knowing our capabilities and limitations, knowing what gives us pleasure and pain, knowing how we uniquely operate, and valuing that uniqueness. Embodiment is being fully aware of our environment and the responses of our body to that environment by being fully conscious and aware and affirmatively responding to life.

Finally we come to learn about our own limits of endurance and survival. We are often capable of much more than we would imagine. There are some good programs like Outward Bound, Project

Adventure, and Ropes Courses that present the individual with risks and challenges that expand the self and the world in wonderful ways. Too often, we are taught not to trust ourselves or our feelings or our minds. Parents can do much to encourage the development of self reliance.

BODY AWARENESS ACTIVITIES

PERFORMANCE OBJECTIVES
By performing these activities and improving his competence over a period of time, your child will have a better awareness of the capacities of his body in general, as well as more awareness of his relationship to the environment. He will come to know what his limits are and he will learn to judge movements and predict outcomes, while becoming prepared for more advanced activities.

1) Obstacle Course
We all need to learn the shape of our bodies, how big we are, how much space we take up, how small a space we can get through. Obstacle courses can be helpful for this. A good obstacle course should include: 1) things to crawl under, like tables or chairs; 2) things to jump over, like benches, sofas, low fences, small flower beds; 3) things to go around, including any kind of furniture; and 4) things to dodge and not touch in close quarters, so your child learns the limits of his body. It will be desirable to indicate which pieces of furniture are to be used for going under, over, or around and in which sequence. Once the

obstacle course is learned, your child can be timed to promote agility and speed. You can also have him start from the end of the course and go backwards to the beginning. Let him time you.

2) Imitation

Stand facing each other, arms out to the side at shoulder level. The leader slowly moves his arms in slightly varying positions by raising or lowering one or both arms. The follower imitates as accurately as possible, mirroring the leader. Allow a short pause in between movements. Switch leader and follower. With practice, add variety and complexity, making the arm movements more elaborate. Add full-body movements. If desired, at some later point, the leader could add music and leg movements so that the imitation would really involve dancing. The objective is for your child to learn to imitate comfortably. Avoid trying to catch each other off guard.

3) Ball Balance

Use a ball of any size and stand facing each other. Place the ball between both of your foreheads (which may require much bending and stretching) and try to keep the ball there without using your hands by gently pressing your foreheads toward each other. If you are successful at that, try moving from one end of the room to the other, still keeping the ball between your foreheads. If you are successful at that, put the ball between your shoulders and

move from one end of the room to the other. Now, put the ball between your hips. Between the outside of your knees. Invent your
own ways.

4) Toesies

Both of you lie down on the floor with
the bottoms of your feet
touching so that the two of
your form one straight line. Attempt to roll across the floor, keeping
the bottoms of your feet touching. Now roll back the same way.
This will cause many laughs.

5) Blind Walk

In a fairly open room, or outside in an open area of lawn or hard
surface, ask your child to close his eyes and get balanced. Then hold
onto his arm and walk with your child. After some practice ask your
child to walk by himself with his eyes closed and you will walk with
him but not touch him, keeping him from hurting himself and telling
him which way to go when he comes to an obstacle. While doing
this ask your child to think about all of the information that he is
getting from all of his sensory systems other than vision. What did
he smell, hear, feel? Could he anticipate where he was? Change
walking and guiding roles.

6) Rag Doll

On a mat, have your child practice falling like a rag doll from a kneel-
ing position. Then have him practice falling from a standing position. You will enjoy this too.

7) Something Going On Inside

Have your child lie down on his back with his eyes closed. For about
one minute ask him to become aware of his breathing rate. Then ask

him to become aware of his heart rate. It may be necessary for him to put the first three fingers of one hand against the neck, right next to the vocal cords to feel a strong pulse. If this is too difficult, have him put his hand over his heart.

8) Contact

Ask your child to contact one part of his body with another and then make variations like:

> hand to knee
> elbow to knee
> hand to nose
> toe to forehead

Make up others that are easy to do.

To make it even more fun, the two of you can try it together so you touch your left elbow to your child's right shoulder, then he touches your left foot with his right knee, etc.

9) Loose Galloose

Have your child relax arm and leg muscles by shaking them. Have him stand with body weight on one foot while shaking the free leg and arms. Then stand on the other leg while shaking the free leg and arms.

10) Robots

Have your child lie on his back with eyes closed. Name a body part and have him move that part of his body gently. Then name other parts and have him respond with gentle movements. Later ask him to make his movements large. Another time make his movements fast or slow. Invent your own ways of moving.

11) Clock Hands

Practice jumping quarter turns and half turns. Play a game in which you give directions for jumping such as half-turn right, quarter-turn left, etc., while your child responds. Then add the dimensions of a clock and have him turn as though he were the center of a clock, facing 4 o'clock, 10 o'clock, and so on.

12) Creepy-Crawly

Both you and your child begin on your hands and knees, with hands directly below shoulders, knees under hips.

Lift up both hands and place them a foot or two forward on the floor, then bring the knees forward until they are below the hips again. Do this several times.

This time, in the same starting position, move right hand and right knee forward a foot or two, then left hand and knee. Do this several times.

This last time, starting in the same position, move your right hand and left knee forward at the same time, then the left hand and the right knee. This kind of crawling can be helpful to walking coordination. Do this several times.

13) Cross The Creek

Draw two parallel lines on the ground or floor about two feet apart to act as the creek. Ask your child to jump or leap across it. If your child has difficulty with this width, make the creek narrower. As he is successful, widen the creek a few inches and take more jumps across it until you reach the limit that your child can jump or leap. These distances should improve with growth and practice.

14) Jump And Reach

Have your child stand with his right side next to a wall that is free of obstacles. Ask him to hold a piece of chalk in his right hand and jump as high as he can and mark the wall with the chalk at his highest reach. This will take some practice. Have him start with his feet together and knees bent so that as he jumps up he does so by extending his legs and ankles and stretches out his body as far up as it will extend. Then you try it. You both should improve with practice.

15) Log Roll

Ask your child to lie down on a mat with his legs straight and arms extended on the floor beyond the head. In this position ask him to roll the length of the mat without rolling sideways off the mat. It will take some practice to roll in a straight line. Once he has succeeded, you try it.

16) The Drawbridge

Ask your child to lie on the floor face up. Have him slowly raise his legs keeping them straight, lowering them over the head until the toes touch the floor. Return slowly to the starting position. Then you lie down opposite him with your toes touching his and raise and lower legs together.

17) Shoulder Stand

Ask your child to lie on his back on the floor, face up; raise the legs with the knees bent, then raise the pelvis, then raise the lower trunk from the floor until the weight is resting on the shoulders, neck and back of the upper arms. Hold the waist with the hands. Do this several times. Then you do it too.

18) Bike Ride

Ask your child to get in the Shoulder Stand position in activity #17 and straighten the right leg vertically in the air while the left leg bends at the knee. Alternate these leg positions so that he is simulating riding a trike or a bike. Try it yourself.

19) Rocking Horse

Ask your child to lie face down with arms outstretched to sides or overhead. Ask him to raise his arms, neck, head, and legs as high as possible. Rock back and forth in this position. You try it.

20) Sit-Ups

Ask your child to lie down, face up with arms at sides and knees bent. Ask him to sit up without using his hands until his forehead touches his knees. It might be helpful for you to hold his feet on the floor. If he is having difficulty, have him do a curl forward as far as he can to get his head and shoulders off the floor and then return to the lying down position. After some practice with this modified version, he should later be able to do the full sit-up and later still, several sit-ups.

21) Push-Ups

Ask your child to lie down, face down with  hands under his shoulders, arms straight, knees bent, with feet in the air. Ask him to push his arms to a straight position so that he lifts his head and shoulders off the ground. Then return to starting position. If he has difficulty, go only half way to the straight arm position and then return to the starting position. You try it.

22) Identifying Body Parts

Have your child close his eyes while you touch a part like the arm and ask him to name that part. Then touch several other parts such as the head, shoulders, elbows, fingers, knees, legs, ankles, feet, stomach, back, hips and other parts as he names them.

23) Identifying Head Parts

As in activity #22, touch your child's nose and ask him to name that part, then touch and name eyes, eyebrows, hair, ears, lips, teeth, chin, neck.

24) Finger Touch

Ask your child to touch all the fingertips of his right hand independently, in succession, with the thumb of the right hand. When this is easy, go in reverse, starting with the index finger. When this is easy, try these activities with the left hand.

Chapter 3

SPATIAL AND TEMPORAL AWARENESS

SPACE/TIME

Most people who have lived long enough to be parents have had sufficient space/time development to know if they can pass the car ahead of them before an oncoming car reaches them. They are able to infer how fast or slow or soon or late they and the other car will be arriving at a particular spot. Most adults know how to pour a cup of coffee or tea without spilling it. They know how to dress themselves before they walk out of the house. These very complex abilities are learned over long periods of time, space and experience. Space and time are the dimensions within which we do our living, experiencing, functioning, and thinking. Participating in the simple things in life like eating, walking, reading, writing, speaking, accomplishing most tasks, involve similar space/time constructions.

For most of us in this country, space and time are separate entities. We measure them differently, by yard sticks, tape measures, road maps, or clocks, calendars and wrinkles. Most of us are unaware at the verbal level that space and time are two sides of the same coin. But let's discuss them separately for a moment.

Space
How much space do you take up? How large is your house?, your yard? How far do you live from the airport? How small is your cat or dog?

When an infant is growing and developing, the only space of interest is the immediate space around her. The space within the reach of a hand or a toe or a mouth is the only space in her world. As the infant learns to creep and crawl, her space expands to the elements she can reach in her room, or the hallway, and eventually, the whole house. This very small world expands as does the infant's perspective, concepts and abilities. Walking makes even more space possible. She can go out into the yard and investigate green, growy things, crawly things, pet the dog, chase the butterfly. Ultimately she will find her way around the block, to the playground, the school, the grocery store. Someday she will go away from home, perhaps to another country. She will think about the possibilities of going to the moon or Mars or some distant galaxy. As we become more and more capable, our universe becomes larger and larger.

Moving toward and away from objects involves specific kinesthetic feedback as well as muscular exertion and relaxation to provide information about the location and distance of objects. Movement provides opportunities to view objects from different perspectives. A doll and a football must be manipulated in order to learn size constancy of these irregular objects.

Time

Time is more mysterious. How did anyone ever invent a clock? How do we know that time passes? Why do we say that time progresses? That time marches on? That time goes forward? What is forward?

Internally, we know that one heart beat follows another, that our breathing is a sequence of inhalations and exhalations. We know that one event takes place before or after another, or at least at some different time. When things happen simultaneously, we often have difficulty figuring them out.

Our rhythms of waking and sleeping, eye blink rate, speech rate, running speed, our biological clocks in general will vary with each individual. When time drags or is going too fast, it can be a matter of our environment, our chemistry, or our DNA. As our capacity to remember increases, we become able to identify that events occur one after another, so that sequencing of events becomes possible.

In order to grasp a glass of milk, a child must first reach toward the glass, reach out her fingers and curl them around the glass, then close the fingers around the glass. The child must have the strength to hold the glass and know when she has exerted enough force to keep it from slipping out of her fingers. She must not exert so much force that she squashes the plastic glass, but enough to hang onto it. Then she must move her hand toward her mouth letting her lips meet the rim smoothly. She must tip the glass upward somewhat, but not too much and swallow the milk as it is poured into her mouth. All this sequencing is very precise and very important and must be done in the appropriate order, or the milk will land on the kid or all over the floor. This is often called timing even though it takes place in space.

SPACE/TIME RELATIONS

Einstein helped us learn that the fourth dimension of space is time; that height, width and depth all take place in time. It is impossible to be some place without regard to time, as it is impossible to be in some time without regard to location. The distance between planets is a matter of time called light years. The distance between San Francisco and Los Angeles is a matter of eight car-driving hours or one plane hour. Learning the relationships between sequencing, linearity, and motion, through space/time is a necessary life construction in order to be efficient and effective in movement, learning and thinking.

When we throw a ball to someone, we estimate the person's movement (time) and the ball's movement (time), the direction of the moving person (space) and the direction of the moving ball (space) and attempt to have the person and the ball arrive at the same place at the same time.

SPACE/TIME ACTIVITIES

PERFORMANCE OBJECTIVES
By performing the following activities and improving her competence over a period of time, your child will develop a better space/time awareness which will help her become more effective, efficient and purposeful in her movement, learning and thinking.

1) Passing The Penny

Get a penny or a dime or a quarter and place it in your right hand. Standing directly in front of your child. Change the penny from your right hand to your left hand. Then put the penny in your child's right hand. Ask her to put it in her left hand and then put it in your right hand. Repeat this several times, until you both become smooth and speedy. Then go in the other direction, from your left hand to your right hand, to your child's left hand and then her right hand.

To make this more difficult, pass the penny from your right index finger to your left index finger, to your child's right index finger, to her left index finger, and so on. Make up your own ways for passing the penny.

2) Penny Ball

While you have the penny, place it on the floor a few feet between you and your child. With almost any kind of ball, bounce pass the ball to your child so that it hits the penny on the bounce and arrives about chest height at your child. Then have your child bounce pass the ball back in the same way. Try to make your passes easy to catch. Then move farther and farther apart with your passing as you master each distance.

3) Rhythm

With your child opposite you, start clapping your hands slowly and rhythmically. Ask her child to clap at the same time you clap. When this is easy, try a little faster rhythm. Then let her set the rhythm and you follow.

Now smile your mouth up and then down rhythmically, and have your child follow you. Blink your eyes rhythmically with her imitating. Ask her to be leader by moving one hand up and down rhythmically. Create your own ways of being rhythmical.

4) Dropping Things

Place an open tin can or open milk carton or pan on the floor. Ask your child to stand above the opening and drop clothespins or marbles or pennies into the opening. Take aim before dropping by lining up one eye with your hand, with the opening.

5) Rolling Things

Place the tin can or milk carton about five feet in front of your child. Ask her to roll a ball at the carton or can so that the ball will touch it. When this becomes easy, move the target farther away.

6) Bean Bags

Give your child a bean bag and take one for yourself. Have her mimic what you do: Toss the bean bag into the air so you can catch it easily with both hands. Toss it from one hand to the other. Throw it higher into the air and clap your hands before you catch it. Make up things to do after throwing it and before catching it.

7) Moving While Throwing And Catching

With the same bean bags, have your child mimic what you do: Start walking slowly and throw the beanbag into the air and catch it. Do it while walking faster. Now throw and catch the beanbag while running slowly. Now, run faster. Try it walking backwards. Make up your own ways of moving while throwing and catching.

8) Adding Distance

With your child about five feet away from you, throw the bean bag underhand and gently to her and ask her to throw it back. As this becomes easy, stand farther and farther apart.

9) Bean Bag Box

Place a cardboard box a few feet away from you and your child and throw the bean bag so that it lands in the box. When this becomes easy move the box farther and farther away.

10) Balloon Race

Blow up one balloon and take turns blowing it across the room until it hits the far wall. When you both have mastered the skills involved, blow up another balloon and race with each other to see who can blow their balloon across the room the fastest. When this becomes easy for both of you, use a straw to blow through. Then use your straw  to make another straw roll across the floor or a tin can roll across the floor or turn a cardboard box in a circle. Create your own races.

11) Jumping

With your child do the following jumping patterns together (jump by

taking off from both feet and landing on both feet):
   Jump in place.
   Jump forward three times.
   Jump backward three times.
   Jump to the right three times, then left three times.
   Jump forward once then backward once, repeat
      three times.
   Jump a quarter turn, then a half turn.

12) <u>Hopping</u>

Hop in the same patterns as activity #11. (Do hopping by taking off from one foot and landing on the same foot.)

Chapter 4

DIRECTIONALITY

INTERNAL DIRECTIONALITY

Each of us is the center of our own universe. The direction of a thing is known in relation to the person looking at it. With all the senses, but especially the kinesthetic receptors in the muscles, tendons, joints, and the semicircular canals in the inner ear, we learn right from left, up from down, front from back, and any variations of these directions. The muscles, tendons and joints have millions of receptors that indicate how much each muscle is contracting or relaxing, and in which directions. They tell us how our bodies are balanced at each joint and, in general, where each segment of our bodies is in relation to every other segment.

An infant learns to locate his mother and turns toward her. He learns to move his eyes appropriately to locate a toy. When he hears a noise he can center his body in that direction. He learns to locate objects in relation to himself and becomes aware of his body in space. He learns appropriate amounts of contraction and relaxation of various parts of his body so that he can reach for a wooden block, grasp it with his hand and fingers, and after further investigation with eyes and mouth, eventually he will learn to let it go by relaxing his hand.

These constructions are important coordinates for use in determining where we are, where others are, and what the relationships are. Most all adults are able to write letters, words, and sentences without thinking about the actual formations of each letter or word. Most adults are able to stand up and turn around and sit back down again without plotting out the physics of such movements. This is the result of our highly developed kinesthetic systems that inform us where our bodies and various parts are in space/time and what it takes to change to other positions and relationships. This kinesthetic sense is our main system for understanding relationships of all kinds.

Children need many opportunities to move in many, many different directions and positionings to learn where they are constantly. Tumbling activities which cause children to be upside down, sideways, rolling, curling, and endless variations of these positions are especially good for developing internal directionality. Swimming is also excellent, especially if the child does lots of tumbling-like activities in the water, standing on hands, somersaults, etc.

A strong sense of internal directionality is essential before the child can learn external directionality.

EXTERNAL DIRECTIONALITY

At about the age of seven, as a result of the further development of the neurons, the social influences of school and the increasing pressure to develop verbal thought, many children learn to apply their internal directionality to the outside world. We learn what arrows mean, where our classroom is in relation to other classrooms, which chair in the room is ours, how to find our way home and the interrelationships between things outside ourselves.

The individual is able to relinquish being the center of the universe and accept an outside center. He can tell that Suzy is standing to the left of John and behind Jane. To some extent, he can learn to walk in another's shoes. He can see his friend, Mikey running down the street and know whether or not he can run fast enough to catch up to him. He can determine which shortcuts to take to intercept him. He can weigh the possibilities before he decides which action to take.

READING

Reading starts at the top of the page, not at the bottom, so the reader must be able to determine where the top is. Reading proceeds from left to right. Words are clumps of letters, the order of which is important in deciphering their meaning.

SAW is not WAS, nor ZVM nor MVZ

p is not q

b is not d

Understanding the differences between right and left and up and down, internally as well as externally, is essential to school success. We learn to apply this knowledge to a horizontal piece of paper on our desks as well as a vertical chalkboard. Reading is a space/time task where the individual applies internal space/time constructs to the external world.

MATHEMATICS

Mathematics is also a space/time task and involves relationships between objects and between details. When playing a simple game of tennis, each time you plan to return the ball, it becomes necessary to compute, unconsciously, at some level, the following: the speed of the ball, the angle of flight, the curvature of fall, direction, rate of progressive decrease of speed, windage, spin, effects of the ball's bounce, how fast and in what direction to move your own body, when to turn your side to the net, start the backswing, shift your weight, execute your backswing with your arm, and start your forward swing in order for the strings of your racket to intercept the ball at the right space/time.

The same complex computations are necessary to some extent for every movement of the body. Of course, very few of us could figure out these specific computations with a paper and pencil, or even a mainframe computer. But, we do compute these specifics internally at an unconscious level. We are truly miraculous beings. Not all of us have had the opportunities to learn to do these things efficiently, yet these computations underlie everything we do.

DIRECTIONALITY ACTIVITIES

PERFORMANCE OBJECTIVES

By performing the following activities and improving your child's competence over a period of time, he will develop a better awareness of personal direction, as well as external and even interpersonal direction, which will prepare him for direction-dependent activities such as reading and math.

1) Marsden Ball

Put a string through a nerf ball so that the ball can be hung from a hook in the ceiling or a doorway or a tree branch. Place the ball so that it is at the child's eye level when he stands facing it.

a) Gently swing the ball to and from your child and have him watch it as it comes and goes.

b) Gently swing the ball from side to side and have him point his finger at the ball as it moves back and forth.

c) Suspend the ball about three feet from the floor, Have your child lie on his back directly under the ball. Swing the ball in large circles as your child watches it until it comes to a stop. Invent different ways to swing the ball while your child watches it.

2) Flashlight

Get a flashlight for each of you and shine your light on the walls and slowly move it around the room. Ask your child to catch your light with his own flashlight. Move in circles, horizontal, vertical and oblique planes. As this becomes easy speed up the movement of the light. Let your child be the leader.

3) Directions

Ask your child to take 4 steps forward, then 4 steps backward, then 4 steps to the right side, then 4 steps to the left side. Then move in these four directions by hopping, jumping, galloping, skipping, on tiptoe, etc.

4) Walking

Ask your child to walk around the area and then call to him some of the following ways you would like him to change his walking pattern.

a)   Take very long, heavy steps.

b)   Take very tiny light steps.

c)   Walk sideways to the right then to the left.

d)   Walk fast or slow.

e)   Walk in Slalom, zigzagging between and around objects.

f)   Walk toeing out, then toeing in.

g)   Walk backwards.

h)   Add your own variations.

5) Running

Ask your child to run slowly around the area and then call out to him the changes you want him to make in his running style. Do just a few of these items at any one time or he will tire too easily.

a)   Run forward, then backward.

b)   Run in a circle to the right, then a circle to the left.

c)   Run along a line.

d)   Run, bringing knees as high up as possible.

e)   Run, kicking your heels back as high as possible, almost kicking your seat.

f)   Run stretched up as high as possible, then run crouched as low as possible.

g)   Run with big arm swings.

h)   Run fast, then run slowly.

i)   Run in a zigzag pattern.

j)   Start running and stop immediately on signal.

6) Keep It Up

Using a balloon, toss it in the air while you and your child take turns batting it up high, trying to keep it from landing on the ground. Try to alternate hits.

7) Target

Make a target using a paper plate or some typing paper and tape it to the wall at about shoulder height. With a soft ball have your child practice throwing underhand from about ten feet from the target. Then put a blindfold on him and ask him to throw at the target ten times.

With each throw, retrieve the ball and advise your child whether the throw was high or low, right or left of the target and by how much. Encourage him to adjust and try to hit the center next time. He should direct the ball with the pads on the ends of his fingers as the ball leaves his hand. Now you do the same thing while your child retrieves and advises on direction.

8) <u>Listening</u>
Ask your child to sit down on the floor and close his eyes. Take a bean bag and throw it gently to the right of your child and ask him to point where he hears the bean bag drop. Then throw it to the left, directly in front and directly in back (hardest). Do this several times until it is easy for him to hear directions.

9) <u>Circles</u>

a)   Ask your child to walk in circles to his right and then to his left.

b)   Ask him to jump in circles to high right and to his left.

c)   Ask him to hop in circles to his right and to his left.

d)   Make up variations.

e)   You try it.

10) Kicker

a)   Ask your child to extend his right arm at about shoulder height in front of him and then kick his right hand with his right foot. If his right hand is too high to be reached, have him lower it so he can kick it.

b)   Have him extend his left arm and kick his left hand with his left foot.

c)   Have him extend his right arm and kick his right hand with his left foot.

d)   Have him extend his left arm and kick his left hand with his right foot.

11) Jumper

Place your child a few feet in front of a wall and gently roll a small ball toward him. Ask him to jump up in the air as the ball rolls under his feet. If he can't jump up very far, ask him to jump forward a little, as well as up, so that he won't land on the ball as it goes under his feet. Retrieve the ball and do this several times. As it becomes easy, roll the ball a little faster. Change roles.

Chapter 5

BALANCE

CENTER OF GRAVITY

Gravity requires that we develop a state of stability or equalization of the body parts about the central pull of gravity's force or we will fall over. When standing erect, the center of gravity is located about an inch or two below the navel. As the body moves so does the center of gravity. It becomes necessary to change the varying relationships of the body parts relative to this gravitational pull to avoid catastrophic results, as the center of gravity changes with each movement. This process often involves stabilizing one part of the body, such as the left leg, while another part, such as the right leg, is in motion, when you are walking. When you are sitting in a chair writing, your legs and trunk must stabilize your body so that you will avoid falling off your chair, as well as free your dominant hand for fluid writing movements.

Eventually, most of us learn to recognize when we are about to fall off the ladder before we actually do and can correct our balance. A good sense of balance makes it possible for us to keep from landing in a heap on a ski run or a tennis court. It makes it possible for a Greg Luganis to move in the exact space/time pattern of superlative Olympic diving.

STABILIZATION

Infants slowly progress from a lying down position with little need to stabilize, to positions that require progressively greater balance.

Even while lying down, infants must stabilize their bodies to some degree so that when reaching for a toy, they won't roll over in the direction of the reaching arm. Infants learn to lift their upper bodies on their arms and later to move to a hands and knees position (four point). Beginning to crawl, they will learn to allow one or two of these support bases to be moved while the others stabilize (three point). Once infants become proficient with crawling that is increasingly bipedal (two points), they become ready to stand. With some experience with upright balancing on two feet (still two point), infants will begin to experiment with unipedal (one point) balance as they stabilize one foot and move the other forward.

It usually takes ten to fifteen months for infants to reach this form of complex balancing. It will take them another three years to develop a stable, fluid, rhythmic walking pattern.

ORIENTATION

The individual who cannot answer complex questions while walking but who can answer complex questions while sitting down has a balance problem. Often such a child finds it necessary to give total attention to how she is walking and has little or no attention left to think about other things. Often such youngsters have not developed space/time relationships and balance skills sufficiently.

Several studies have shown significant positive correlations between balance abilities and reading speed and comprehension abilities at second and third grade levels. We also know that in order to write, we must have the strength to hold and manipulate a pencil or crayon. In addition to that, we must have the strength and balancing ability to sit up in a chair and not fall off, hold up our head, move fingers, wrist, hand and arm in a coordinated fashion while thinking about what it is that we wish to write. Writing is an asymmetrical task. Several parts of the body stabilize while one segment manipulates.

Our kinesthetic receptors in the muscles, tendons and joints are our main senses giving us information about balancing. Touch is also helpful, especially against supporting surfaces like the soles of our feet. The semicircular canals in our inner ears also keep the head aligned in terms of its position in relation to gravity. And vision gives us information about our bodies in relation to other objects. During the constantly changing conditions of walking, running, jumping, twirling and somersaulting, our capacity for balance keeps us apprised of where we are and where we are moving to next.

BALANCE ACTIVITIES

PERFORMANCE OBJECTIVES

By performing the following activities and improving your child's competence over a period of time, she will develop a better sense of balance that will allow her to concentrate on other activities such as reading and writing without having to consciously think about the balance of any part of her body. She will become more graceful and fluid in her movement activities as well.

1) Balancing On Head

Have your child put a ruler on her head and try to balance it there. When this is easy, try a yardstick or a book. Try it with a bean bag. Now ask her to walk forward while balancing the beanbag. Then backward. Make up your own ways to balance.

2) Tiptoes And Heels

Ask your child to stand on her tiptoes and balance there as long as she can. Then ask her to balance on her heels as long as she can. When this is successful, ask her to walk around the room on her tiptoes for awhile and then walk around on her heels.

3) One Leg Balance

Ask your child to stand on one foot and bend forward, raising the free leg backward until the trunk and free leg are parallel to the floor. Have her hold her arms out at right angles to her body. Repeat on the other leg. Have her balance on one leg with the trunk and arms in different positions, sideways, backwards, making up her own creations. See how long she can hold these balanced positions.

4) One Leg Swing

Ask your child to balance on one foot and swing the free leg forward and backward. Try it on the other leg. Then try it first swinging the free leg forward then sideward, then backward. Try it on the other leg.

5) Stepping Stones

Using chalk on the pavement or a concrete surface, draw a series of circles a foot or two apart, like stepping stones. Ask your child to step from one stone to the next forward and then backward. Make the stepping stones farther and farther apart. Create your own ways of doing this.

6) Walk The Line

Draw or tape a line on the ground and ask your child to walk along it, then walk it backwards, then sideways, then skipping, hopping, and jumping. Make up your own ways to travel on the line.

7) Jumping

Ask your child to jump over the line you have drawn or taped on the floor. Then put a rope down on the floor and ask her to jump over that. Then get a small box for her to jump over, and a larger one when all these things become easy. Have your child jump up and down stairs, one step at a time.

8) Tripod

This is a lead up to the head stand so be prepared to catch your child if she topples over. On a mat or soft rug or soft lawn, ask her to kneel down on her hands and knees. Then ask her to place her head on the ground in front of her hands so the hands and head form a triangle. Then ask her to walk her feet slowly up toward her hands forcing her seat up higher and higher into the air. When her knees come pretty close to her elbows, ask her to first place one knee on her elbow with the foot off the floor and then the other knee on the other elbow with the foot off the floor. This will work only if she has forced her seat forward so that it is directly over her head when she puts her knees on her elbows. Do this several times until she can maintain this tripod position for a minute or so, with her feet off the floor.

9) Head Stand

When your child is successful with the tripod position ask her to slowly raise her legs up into the air until they are straight and her body is straight (not arched). If the tripod has worked for her, this should also work. Have her try it several times until she can balance in a head stand for one minute. Your turn.

10) Walking Board

a)   Find a handy 2" x 4", 6 to 8 feet long without splinters, and place it on level ground with the wide edge down. Have your child walk slowly forward on the board from one end to the other.

b)   Then walk the board backward.

c)   Then walk sideways one length with the right leg leading and one length with the left leg leading.

d)   Practice these skills several times slowly. Later have your child focus her vision on some distant object about shoulder height while doing all these different directions

e)   Now make creative additions like:
         walking on tiptoe
         with a beanbag on your head
         crawl across the board
         turn around on the board
         toss a beanbag up in the air and catch it while walking

Chapter 6

BODY CONCEPT AND SELF-ESTEEM

BODY CONCEPT

Each person's body concept involves primarily how the person values his body, its parts and its functioning. Certainly, body awareness is also involved, but body awareness is the knowledge of the body, often at unconscious levels, while body concept is the goodness or badness that we attribute to the body, how well we like or dislike our physical being. The way a person looks, the way he moves, the way he grins or frowns, the way he dresses and grooms himself, and the ways in which he chooses not to move or appear, constitute some of the ways in which a person values himself. The way you feel about your body affects the way you feel about all the other aspects of your self. Body concept is acquired and therefore can be changed, especially by the positive influence of parents and teachers.

The body is the first self-concept that we have. And, for awhile it is inseparable from our environment. Our mother is part of us, our crib, our blanket. With body experience we begin to learn that we have a separate self.

The body is the only tangible thing that we have. We can touch it, feel it, move it and get to know it as "mine" or "me".

PARENTAL INFLUENCES

Parents influence the body concepts of their youngsters in many very specific ways. If a parent does not like her body, or bodies in general, or touching in particular, it will directly affect the child's valuing of his body. Each infant is a part of his mother's body concept and, now increasingly, his father's body concept. If the parents are reasonably secure and comfortable about who they are and what they do, they will extend that security and comfort to their child. If they are insecure, however, they will project that insecurity onto their child.

CULTURAL INFLUENCES

Our culture teaches parents to treat each child differently depending on whether it is male or female. Today we can tell the sex of a fetus before it is born and often parents are treating the yet-to-be-born offspring by its gender. Many mothers let the fetus listen to classical music or football cheers. Many mothers choose to be physically active or sedentary. She talks differently to her male fetus than she does to her female fetus.

After birth, the baby's room may be painted blue or pink. The clothes may be color coordinated. There are dolls and frills or footballs and trains at hand. Studies have shown that girls will be looked at and talked to more than boys. Girls have better hearing acuity at birth than boys. Girls will be touched and handled more than boys, probably because it is OK for girls to be gentled. Boys will be encouraged to get off the lap much sooner and explore the world and become independent as soon as possible. Boys will be encouraged to be more physical and rough.

Physical abilities are important to both sexes. All children enjoy mastery over such things as being able to dress themselves, tie their shoes, button shirts, ride their trike, then bike, win races, and fights. Subtle differences begin to take place as children grow up, with girls becoming graceful while boys become athletic. But, certainly, driving a car, swimming, dancing, and being an efficient mover, instead of a klutz, are important to both sexes.

Most parents make great attempts to be certain that their child has learned the appropriate gender role before he or she gets to school, whether this is politically correct today or not. By puberty, girls are usually taught something about the problems of being sex objects. They often learn to be aware of sexual connotations that others will put on their behavior, no matter how innocent. And they must learn to interpret other's behaviors toward them so as to avoid difficulty with ulterior motives. Girls learn to double-think in social situations. Girls learn that their individuality and their sexuality are the same thing. It is a difficult line to draw between being sexually attractive and being open to sexual promiscuity. Parents can be especially helpful in giving their daughters the confidence to avoid sexual advances until they reach adulthood.

Parents can also provide confidence for their sons so that they do not have to prove themselves in ways that hurt themselves or others. Parents can help their sons learn the qualities of gentleman versus machoman so that they can consider the advantages and disadvantages of each.

Girls are permitted to be more experimental with appearance and clothing, while boys are permitted to be more experimental with extremes of physical performance.

Families tend to teach their children that the characteristics of their clan are the most desired. So, in some families, dark hair and brown eyes are more highly valued than light hair and blue eyes, and vice versa. Strong chins, high foreheads, small ears, or just the reverse become the ways of identifying one's own from the other.

Sometimes parents will teach goodness or badness of a body part or function. Badness is more apt to be connected to the genitalia and sexual functioning or parts of the body that either don't perform up to some standard or don't look quite right. Goodness usually becomes associated with those parts that are approved of as especially attractive.

And then our culture and the media take over. We are taught through television, magazines, and books, that being white, male, tall, strong, are the most desired qualities. Anything else is lacking. Handsome and beautiful people fill our TV screens. Lean, agile bodies are the usual for the heroes and heroines. Villains come in poorly proportioned shapes often with disfigured or asymmetrical angry faces, indicating what we are supposed to disapprove of. Parents can help their children understand the limitations and narrowness of the media and aid in discounting many of these negative stereotypes.

The media and all the beauty and fitness industries make it almost impossible for any of us to be happy with ourselves if we are overweight. Girls and women especially believe that they must be thin to be liked by others. This is affecting our youngsters at earlier and earlier ages. For years, many of us believed that it was sinful to be fat. Fat people got what they deserved. Many of us believed that fat people had no will power and could not control themselves.

We now know that this is not true. There are many elements that lead to becoming overweight. There are many psychological elements, not the least of which is lack of self-esteem and self-worth. There are many genetic elements that predispose many to have low metabolic rates and efficient use of nutrients. There are many environmental elements like sedentary jobs and limited exercise opportunities. For almost a century it was believed that thin people were healthier and lived longer. Research is now underway that may establish the advantages of being 5 to 10% overweight in extending the length of life.

We now know that many industries make unbelievably large amounts of money because many of us are insecure about weighing too much. We need to invent industries that will make unbelievably large amounts of money because many of us are insecure about weighing too little. Or, at least, industries that don't care what we weigh. More important, people need to be aware of the manipulations of such industries and not allow themselves or their families to be influenced by them.

GROWING UP AND OLDER

As children grow up and as adults grow old, they are never sure what they will become. Children worry about ultimate breast size, penis size, whether they will be tall or short, broad-shouldered, fat, thin, handsome, beautiful. We need to let our children know that it is the person that they are and the things that they do that are the important things in life. Conformation to society's dictates of appearance are really not important to the contributions one can make to life on this planet.

We need to teach our children to trust their bodies. They need to learn to depend on themselves, not drugs, not intimidation, not force. They need to learn the limitations of their bodies as well as their capacities and appreciate what they can do well. If there is something they really don't like, they should either change it, if it is possible, or forget it, if it is not possible to change safely. Our children need to be secure in their bodies, comfortable to try out new things, unafraid to make fools of themselves on occasion. They need to be comfortable in their own sex, without needing to distort, exaggerate or hide their sexuality.

Children will learn primarily from their parents and somewhat from their culture how attractive or unattractive they are. They will learn how large or small, how strong or weak, how masculine or feminine, how capable or incapable they are and in what ways. These understandings of themselves will have considerable influence on the ways they will dress, groom, exercise, diet, camouflage, choose friends, choose careers, choose mates, choose risks, and enjoy or despair of life.

We all need to learn that people vary in how we experience the world, how we behave as men and women, how we relate to others. The experiences of each person are different from every other person. We all inhabit different sensory worlds. Different languages and cultures also affect how we move and how we think. If you can make your child aware of how different we all are and that it is good to be different, you will help him to appreciate himself. In some ways he will know how different he is more than you do. It is only through our differences that we can contribute to the rest of society, especially in a democracy.

Most researchers view the self-concept as the most important single factor in determining human behavior and performance. And parents play a crucial role in helping children develop a self-concept that is tolerant of difference and satisfied with the self as it is.

BODY CONCEPT ACTIVITIES

PERFORMANCE OBJECTIVES

By performing the following activities and improving your child's competence over a period of time, he will develop a better concept of his body, thereby leading to a better self-concept and improved self-esteem. He will learn to appreciate and value his own differences as well as the differences of others.

1) Drawing The Body

Get two pieces of butcher paper or newsprint, larger than one's body. Have the child lie down on the paper while you trace an outline of his body around the outside edges of his body with a pencil or crayon. Have him do the same for you. Then as humorously as possible have your child draw clothes on the drawing of his body while you do the same on your drawing. Add eyes, ears, nose, mouth. Admire each other's work. Talk about each body part and encourage your child to name them. Then, think about how big each body is, where it begins and ends, how long the arms are, how long the legs are, how big the head is. Talk about each body shape in general. Hang the pictures on the wall and treasure them.

2) Height And Weight

Measure your child's height and weight and keep a chart indicating growth.

3) Pictures

Take pictures of your child and look at them together, pointing out specific characteristics such as hair, eyes, expression, size, etc.

4) Video Camcorder

If possible, rent or buy a video camcorder and videotape your children often and talk positively about their appearance and all the good things they can do. The more knowledgeable your children are in regard to their bodies, the easier it will be for them to deal with the attitudes and opinions of others as they go through life.

5) Variety

Give your children opportunities to do many different kinds of things. The more versatile they can become the more choices they will have throughout life.

6) Talk With Your Child

Ask your child such things as: What parts of your body do you think are attractive? Why do you think this? What parts do you think are ugly? Why do you think this? How does TV affect the way you think about attractiveness? What are your good traits that you would like to keep and maybe enhance? What are your negative traits that you would like to eliminate? What things about your physical appearance do you want to change? Are they changeable? Discuss accepting things that are not changeable.

7) Personalize

Ask your child to decorate his own room or at least a corner of it.

Have this be a perpetual project that involves adding new things that are important at the time and removing old things that no longer have interest.

8) <u>Sensory Awareness</u>

Ask your child to experiment with enhanced or diminished sensory input. Put a blindfold on him and let him get to know his room or the whole house without the use of vision. Be careful to help him keep from stumbling or hurting himself. Put earplugs or cotton in his ears and have him listen to music or TV and note the differences from normal hearing. Put aerobic weights on his ankles and wrists for a few minutes to an hour and ask him to be aware of how much more musculature it takes to do various things. Add a heavy backpack to your child so he can understand what it is like to carry extra weight.

9) <u>Mirrors</u>

Have at least one full length mirror in the house. Encourage your child to look at himself and experiment with different posturing, expressions, clothing. Ask him if the mirror shows what people are like on the inside. Do this with boys as well as girls.

Chapter 7

MASTERY

We all need to become scientists of our own bodies and minds and spontaneously experiment and experience over and over again. The process of discovery for the child is similar to the process of discovery for the scientist exploring the principles that rule the workings of one's own world. This means being in touch with our own experiences, connected to our own feelings, and having attachments to our own environment. We need to become aware and observant of events in our lives and their consequences for ourselves and others.

EXPERIENCE

In order to find out about the properties of things, one must act on them. There is little to learn about a ball just by looking at it. We must pick it up, squeeze it, drop it, roll it on the floor, throw it in the air, bounce it on the floor, bounce it on the grass, throw it against a wall, drop it down a stairway, kick it, etc. in order to find the properties of a ball. We must learn to manipulate the things in our environment in order to find out what they are. And, we must pay attention to and experience ourselves in order to find out what we can do.

These kinds of experiences help us to structure our world and find order in the chaos. The more rich and varied the experiences, the more accurately we will be able to construct our world. These developmental activities are extremely important for preschool children because their later relationships will be built on the ones that were created earlier. They are indispensable for the later construction of all knowledge. Children can also find security in being able to manipulate objects, controlling them and assessing results.

COMPETENCE

Having developed some mastery in body awareness, space/time awareness, directionality, balance, and self-esteem, more total body mastery is in order.

Being comfortable with oneself is also important. Understanding the miracle of the body is an element in creating this comfort. Living intentionally and deliberately instead of haphazardly requires this basic understanding.

We can always become more competent and sophisticated in everything we do through learning and experience. Most of us tend to like to do the same skills over and over again, like free throw shooting in basketball, because they are fun and because we can do them. But to stay at that level and not learn the other skills of the game is to stunt our lives. Certainly, it takes more concentration and effort to learn new things, but once learned they can be even more fun than the few skills already know. We all need encouragement to try new things, especially if it means failing for awhile. We were all beginners once, in everything. We all need to learn to concentrate, especially when the outcome of an activity is important to us.

And we can always learn more about strategy. Good players of any life game should be able to think of at least two, preferably three or more alternatives for any given situation. There are always new strategies and alternatives to consider. Most strategy involves pre-planning what the possibilities are and their circumstances.

We all need to learn a sense of independence, how to take care of ourselves. When we are small, just learning to get dressed, eat without spilling too much, get around the house without knocking things over are starters. Later we need to know that we can get along in the world and even help others. Ultimately we all need to be confident enough to realize that no matter what may confront us, we will be able to deal with it with skill and success.

Realizing our own outer limits can be challenging and immensely satisfying. There are many programs designed to accomplish these things in the out of doors, such as the Girl and Boy Scouts, Camp Fire, Project Adventure, Ropes Courses, and Outward Bound. These programs not only teach the basics of the outdoors and self-sufficiency but they also teach caution, safety, and the capacity to delight in one's surroundings. The elements of risk and adventure and new challenges are constantly present in most nature activities. Learning how to learn involves adapting to new situations and changing one's perspective and ways of thinking.

As the infant experiences herself and her environment and develops small capacities for reaching a toy or grasping a rattle or getting a wooden block into her mouth, she becomes delighted with her new found capacities and repeats them over and over again. This is the basis of self-mastery as well as self-esteem. This satisfaction and repetition eventually lead to more complex learnings, such as learning to write, run, play games or use a computer.

MAPS OF THE UNIVERSE

To construct an effective map of the world, youngsters must have a great variety of movement activities to experience and repeat at great length. It will take most children at least three years, from age 1 to age 4 of intense practice to develop an efficient, fluid walking pattern. The same is true for most other movement patterns, although many of them are learned later in life. Body-mastery is the first component of self-mastery.

INTERRELATIONSHIPS

Sensing, moving, and thinking are interrelated. They all improve as the individual interacts with the environment and has numerous opportunities to repeat new skills. We can all learn to perceive finer and finer distinctions. We learn a tune played on a piano but can recognize it when it is played on a guitar. We recognize the sound of the piano even when it plays a different tune. We can refine our movements and become excellent drivers, bikers, and even tightrope walkers. Not only can we tell the difference between lifting a ten pound weight and a one pound weight, we can tell the difference between lifting a large feather and a small feather.

Mastery is having confidence that is based on competence. Feeling good about yourself takes many forms, but competence produces much more lasting esteem.

MASTERY ACTIVITIES

PERFORMANCE OBJECTIVES
By performing the following activities and improving your child's competence over a period of time, she will develop mastery over her own body thereby producing competence, independence, and lasting self-esteem which will lead to more complex learnings such as writing, playing games, using a computer and meeting challenges.

1) Walks
Take walks together. Encourage your youngster to investigate anything of interest. The walks don't have to be long but should be intriguing. Check out the kinds of flowers that grow in your neighbors' yards, how many steps it takes to get to the corner, and what kinds of birds are out that day. Examine the bugs and weeds in the street or sidewalk, discuss each different kind of car parked along the way and what makes them different, different kinds of houses, changes in the weather, and on and on.

2) Maps
Have your child make a map of your house, showing each room and

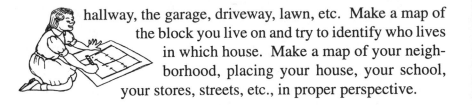 hallway, the garage, driveway, lawn, etc. Make a map of the block you live on and try to identify who lives in which house. Make a map of your neighborhood, placing your house, your school, your stores, streets, etc., in proper perspective.

3) Measuring

Using a tape measure or a ruler or yardstick, have your child measure things of interest: the table, the chair, the TV, the room, the car, etc. Then practice guessing how long or wide an item is. Measure it and see how close you have come.

4) Sculpting

Get some playdough or modeling clay and both of you form figures of people, animals, houses, cars, etc. Talk about the shapes of things and the feel of your fingers on the clay while you are each shaping something. Eventually sculpt a self portrait of your own head and face, using a mirror. These kinds of activities help develop kinesthetic awareness. You can make your own play dough by mixing 2 cups flour, 1 cup salt, 1 tablespoon salad oil, 3/4 cup of water until smooth. Add food coloring, if you like, and store in a plastic bag in the refrigerator. If you create something you really want to save, you can dry it in the oven at 250 degrees Fahrenheit until it is dry.

5) Rope Jumping

a) Place a rope on the ground and ask your child to jump over it with both feet at once.

b) Have your child start on two feet and land on one foot.

c) Tie one end of the rope to a chair or table leg and with you holding the other end, raise the rope an inch or two from the

ground while your child jumps over the rope.

d)   Swing the rope slowly back and forth while your child jumps over it.

e)   Give your child a short rope about three feet long and ask her to swing it back and forth, then up and over her head then back over her head to the beginning position.

f)   Ask your child to swing the rope all the way around, from behind her feet to in front of her feet and to jump as the rope comes in front of her feet. Try for success with just one jump at a time.

g)   When one jump becomes easy, try for two, then three, etc.

h)   Your turn.

6) Ball Handling

Using nerf balls or playground balls or soft beach balls, one ball per person, you and your child should hold the ball in front at chest height. Practice each of the following slowly until it is comfortable and then go on to the next activity. Use the pads on the ends of your fingers rather than the palms of your hands when you are holding, throwing or catching the ball:

a)   Roll the ball around in your hands to get a feeling for its texture, its size and its weight.

b)   Roll the ball around your waist.

c)   Roll the ball around your neck.

d)   Roll the ball around your ankles.

e) Gently toss the ball from one hand to the other.

f) Gently toss the ball in higher loops from one hand to the other.

g) Toss the ball high, straight up into the air and catch it with both hands by pulling it into your chest.

h) Drop the ball and catch it as it comes back up off the ground. Drop the ball and catch it several times.

i) Bounce the ball by pushing it toward the ground with fingertips and then catch it on the rebound.

j) Bounce the ball several times in a row (dribbling).

k) Dribble the ball forward and then backward, slowly and then speed it up a little.

l) Stand facing each other about 10 feet apart, crouch, and slowly roll the ball to your child. Ask her to move into the ball's path and catch it. Then ask her to roll the ball back to you. Try to roll the ball so it is easy to intercept at first. Then roll the ball a little to one side and then to the other, so your child has to move to the proper side to intercept it.

m) Stand facing each other about 10 feet apart and gently throw the ball underhand back and forth to each other. Try to make your throws easy to catch.

n) Catch with your fingers angled sideways away from the ball, while your arms are reaching toward the ball. Grasp the ball with both hands as it comes to you and pull it in toward your body.

o) As this distance becomes easy, increase the distance.

p) When underhand throwing is easy, try over-
hand throwing. Have your child wind up
by taking the ball back, away from the target (you) with one hand while she turns her
other side toward you. Be sure she has her
elbow back away from the target on the wind up. Then have her
unwind by quickly bringing the ball forward, toward you, re-
leasing it as it passes her ear with her fingers the last things to
contact the ball. She should reach out toward you with that
same arm, as the ball is leaving her hand.

q) As your child gets more and more successful, increase the distance of the throwing.

r) Invent your own ways of interacting with balls. Be creative.
Have fun.

7) <u>Rhythmic Planning</u>

Ask your child to lie down on her back while you beat out a slow
even rhythm with a pencil against a table, a drum or even use a met-
ronome or play some even rhythm music. Ask your child to respond
to every beat with each of the following movements, for eight beats.
Say what your child is to do next when you reach the eighth beat.

a) Open your mouth on one beat and close your mouth on the
next.

b) Wiggle your nose to right on one beat and to the left on the
next.

c) Blink both of your eyes.

d) Wink your right eye.

e)   Wink your left eye.

f)   Hunch your right shoulder.

g)   Hunch your left shoulder.

h)   Hunch both of your shoulders.

i)   Breathe in on one beat and out on the next.

J)   Bend your right knee, while keeping your foot on floor on the first beat and straighten your knee on the next beat.

k)   Bend your left knee, while keeping your foot on floor on the first beat and straighten your knee on the next beat.

l)   Bend both of your knees while keeping your feet on the floor on the first beat and straighten on the next.

m)   Bend your right knee on the first beat and your left knee on the next, straightening one of your legs as the other leg bends.

n)   Move your right arm from the side of your body, sliding over the floor until your hand is above your shoulder, on the floor, on one beat and return your arm to the side of your body on the next.

o)   Move your left arm from the side of your body, sliding over the floor until your hand is above your shoulder, on the floor, on one beat and return the arm to the side of your body on the next.

p)   Move your right arm to above your shoulder position on the first beat and your left arm to above your shoulder position on the next, returning each arm to the side as your other arm moves to above your shoulder position.

q) Bend your right knee and move your right arm to your shoulder position on the first beat and bend your left knee and your left arm to your shoulder position on your next beat.

r) Now bend your right knee and move your left arm to your shoulder position on the first beat

 and bend your left knee and move your right arm to your shoulder position on the next beat.

s) Now you try it. As you both become successful, the tempo can be increased.

t) Make up your own versions.

8) Relaxation

This is my version of Jacobson's Progressive Relaxation. This technique is based on learning the difference between tension and relaxation in all parts on your body. Ask your child to lie down on her back while you read the following instructions:

a) Relax as much as possible. Feel yourself sink into the floor.

b) Breathe in slowly and out slowly while you think about your breathing.

c) Every time you breathe in, let your stomach rise up and every time you breathe out let your stomach drop down toward the floor. This is called abdominal breathing and helps in relaxation. When we are tense, usually our chest rises up and down as we breathe in and out. Inhale down deep into your abdomen and feel the rush of air in and out of your nose or mouth. Breathe in a very deep breath while your stomach slowly rises and then exhale very slowly while your stomach slowly lowers. (Repeat this procedure three times.)

d) Clench the fist of your right hand and tighten all the muscles of your arm clear up to your shoulder. Feel what it is like to be so tense. Now relax your whole arm and feel what relaxation is like. Start to learn the difference between tension and relaxation. (Repeat this procedure three times.)

e) (Repeat activity " d " above with the left arm.)

f) Curl the toes of your right foot up and tighten all the leg muscles from your feet clear up to the bottom of your stomach. Feel the tension in your right leg. Now, relax the whole leg and feel the relaxation. Feel the difference between tension and relaxation. (Repeat this procedure three times.)

g) (Repeat activity " f " with the left leg.)

h) Count to ten slowly and loudly and feel the tension that exists in your mouth, tongue and voice box. Now rest and feel how different it is to relax those areas. Repeat this procedure three times. It will even work when counting inaudibly to yourself.

i) Check your arms and legs and breathing and be sure you're relaxed all over.

j) Close your eyes very tightly and feel all the tension created around your eyes. Now relax and feel the difference around your eyes. Repeat three times.

k) (Now you try it.)

If your child is not completely relaxed or asleep, you could start the whole procedure over again. This is a technique that should be mastered so that eventually you and your child can relax in an instant, with one relaxing breath. You both should be able to use this in a number of situations: when you yell at your child or your child yells at you, when the dog bites you, when you have to perform before an audience, etc. With practice you and your child can learn to do this kind of relaxation while sitting or standing in a matter of seconds while doing one large abdominal breath slowly in and out.

9) Jungle Gym
Playing on a jungle gym will increase your child's perception of space, time and directionality, climbing in many different directions and positions. If one is available in your town or school a visit or two is in order.

10) Scooters, Tricycles, Bicycles
Learning to ride on scooters, tricycles, and bicycles will help develop your child's balancing abilities as well as space/time and directionality processes. All of them are worth investing in when your child reaches the appropriate age for each.

11) Kicking

a) Place a playground ball or nerf ball on the ground directly in front of both of your child's feet and ask her to kick the ball. Note which foot she uses because that will usually be the dominant foot while the other foot will be the holding foot.

b) Move about 10 feet in front of her and ask her to gently kick the ball to you. Then you stop it with your hands and gently kick it back to her. Ask her to stop it with her  hands and place the ball in front of her dominant foot and kick it back to you.

c) When the stationary kick is easy, roll the ball to your child and ask her to gently kick it back to you. Then ask her to roll the ball to you and you gently kick it back to her. When this is easy, roll the ball faster.

d) Ask your child to place the ball on the ground, back up a few steps and then run two or three steps up to the ball and gently kick it to you. Then you place it on the ground a few steps in front of you and take two or three steps and gently kick the ball to her.

e) When all these skills become easy, you both can increase the strength of your leg swing when kicking and try to kick farther and farther and with more force. If you have a lot of space, practice kicking for distance and accuracy.

f) Invent new ways to kick.

12) <u>Have Fun!</u>

Chapter 8

UNDERSTANDING OUR BODYMIND

The more you understand about how your body and mind develop, the more you will be able to help yourself and others develop as fully as possible. Humans are born with more flexibility and fewer reflexes than other animals. We are dependent on our parents for a much longer period of time while we learn to use the miraculous potentials we have at birth. Most of us have forgotten the thousands of tiny learning increments we have added to our repertoires moment by moment, day by day to become capable and successful human adults. This chapter will introduce the basic equipment we are born with and how it is used.

CENTRAL NERVOUS SYSTEM

The central nervous system includes the body's mechanisms of receiving and integrating information and then sorting, systematizing and making decisions about this information, and then acting on those decisions. The central nervous system includes such things as the brain, the sensory systems, the movement systems and the feedback systems.

Our sensory systems--tasting, smelling, seeing, hearing, touching, manipulating, and moving--are our vehicles for receiving information from our environment and from our own internal activities. There are many more senses than just five senses, often referred to in older psychology books. It is the information that we receive from these sensory systems that determine what we can know. They serve as the interface between ourselves and our environment.

The neuron is the main building block of the central nervous system and we have over 200 billion of them. The main task for neurons is to communicate with other neurons. Neurons communicate information such as the presence of elements in our environment, or conditions that might need regulation inside our bodies such as temperature, growth of cells, stress, nutrition, etc. Neurons receive electrochemical messages from neighboring neurons and when a stimulation threshold is reached, the neuron releases a transmitter fluid into the synaptic gap to the next neuron. Each neuron has a membranous cell wall that will receive only certain shaped molecules that fit through its particular design. Even as we sleep, several thousand neurons are sending messages from one end of the central nervous system to the other in a matter of milliseconds.

Receptors are collections of neurons that have developed direct connections with the environment, like the eyes and ears. Receptors transmit the nature of the stimuli, such as light, sound, taste or smell. Their messages indicate the intensity of the stimuli such as how strong the odor, how much light, how loud the sound. Receptors translate how long the stimuli are occurring as well as where in the body it is generated. Receptors interpret the language of the environment into the language of the body. They translate external energy into internal energy that travels to specific receiving areas in the central nervous system.

External energy is received by the receptors in the eyes, ears, nose, mouth, skin, muscles, joints, tendons, etc., and is sent via neurons to various parts of the brain for processing. Once a decision is made to act, neurons send messages to the appropriate musculature and behavior occurs, such as fight or flight, hug or kiss, speak or sing or ask for more information. This miraculous process provides us with information that enables us to use the environment to direct our lives safely and happily.

The brain functions primarily to transform the pattern of sensory experience into patterns of movement response. Movement, planning, and evaluations are dealt with primarily in the frontal lobe of the brain. Body sensing is controlled primarily in the top of the brain. Hearing is received in the areas along the sides of the brain. Seeing is interpreted in the very back of the brain.

EXPERIENCE AND DEVELOPMENT

We slowly learn to make interpretations about what is happening externally and internally. We construct our own world so that it correlates with our experience. When something new and different happens that does not match our previous experience, we experiment with it and we compare it to immediate short-term memories and to long-term memories. We may find that we need to change the way we have constructed the world in order to account for this new experience, and we continue to change our constructions of reality throughout life.

All experience is sensory. Although many experiences are verbal and involve words, they come to us through reading which involves the eyes and movement of the eyes and head, or listening, which involves the ears, the muscles that rotate the head, or braille which involves the tactual endings in the finger pads and the musculature that manipulates the fingers and the hands.

We also learn spatial relations between things and their locations. We learn timing and sequencing and learn to coordinate movements so that the body or hand moves to the right space at the right time. We learn to recognize toys, the sound of the door, the smell of our mother, the movement necessary to turn over, and we develop ideas that help us deal with and interact with our world. We repeat most of these interactions thousands of times as our perceptions take on clarity and organization.

Infants must discover how to move an arm or hand in order to grasp a desired object. They select from their repertoire of movements and graspings that have already been developed. It will eventually become necessary to combine arm and leg movements into a plan to get where they want to go. With time and experience, infants improve in their ability to reach, grasp, crawl, walk, and find their way in the world. As more and more of these patterns become available at an automatic level, planning becomes more rapid and fluid. Complex levels of planning will become more analytical and sophisticated as experience becomes more varied.

THINKING AND MOTOR PLANNING: KINESTHESIA

Motor planning eventually leads to thinking at more abstract levels and involves considering and assessing concepts into different combinations in the central nervous system before choosing one plan and acting on it. Because we can do this in milliseconds, we often have time to make the best choices.

A magnificent sensory system that makes movement of any kind possible and is the basis for understanding how the body operates is called kinesthesia. Kinesthesia includes millions of sensory receptors in the muscles, joints, and tendons that supply information about compression and tension of muscles, contraction and relaxation, degrees of angulation of the joints of the body segments and the rate at which the angulation changes. We are able to determine where our different body parts are in space and time and how they are moving in relation to each other and the environment. If we see something we want, we can translate visual space/time into kinesthetic space/time and stand up, walk across the room, and reach out with one hand and pour coffee into a cup held in the other hand. Kinesthesia allows us to do just about anything.

Kinesthesia is the mystery sensory system because it does not stick out like the nose on your face, or your eyes or ears or mouth or skin. Kinesthesia is nestled into the fibers of the muscles and joints and tendons and ligaments. It is hidden from view. These millions of sensory neurons are stimulated every time you move and they send messages to the brain in a matter of milliseconds. Although the other senses were recognized as much as 2,400 years ago, kinesthesia was not clearly recognized as a sensory system until a little over 100 years ago.

An easy way to demonstrate how kinesthesia works is to ask you to put your hands behind your back. Now, make your hands and fingers into something that resembles tiger claws. And now, relax your hands. If you went through this procedure, how do you know that you made your hands into tiger claws, without peeking? Your kinesthetic sense tells you.

As we discover more and more about our bodies and our environment, we are enlarged physically and mentally. The world grows larger as we learn more and more.

FIGURE/GROUND

Since we are surrounded by thousands of stimuli impinging on each sensory system at any one moment, it is important to learn to sense with a focus. When I look out my window, I can focus on the barn in the foreground or the trees in the distance, the red-tailed hawk in the sky or the tiny clover flower in the extremely near greenery. When I focus on the tiny clover flower, it becomes "figure" and everything else becomes background ("ground"). Selecting what to focus on, and in the process, what to omit is necessary for control of input and selective data-gathering. This process of focusing and exclusion is called "figure/ground". Being able to focus on important elements and omit everything else allows us to understand some of the events going on around us. Without this capacity we cannot understand much of anything, for we would be surrounded by chaos.

An infant learns to select his mother to focus his eyes on even though there may be several people in the environment. An infant learns to smell his mother, even though there may be many different aromas to choose from. An infant learns to hear his mother's voice and omit other voices, music, motors, etc. An infant learns to focus all his sensory systems on his mother, making his mother the center of attention for all input.

We do similar kinds of focusing all our lives. When we are driving to work, we see the road and the cars in front of us with greater focus than the houses or grocery stores. We can pick out the French horn from the trumpet when listening to the symphony. We are especially aware of our feet and legs when jumping across a creek, rather than noticing what our hands and fingers are doing. When we have eaten too much, we feel the tight belt around our middle, but pay no attention to the feel of the rest of our clothing on our skin. All of our sensory systems must develop this capacity for figure/ground if we are to live effectively, because it makes perception possible even though it limits how much we can know at any one time.

INTEGRATION

We can generalize common qualities in one sensory system and apply that generalization in a different sensory system. All of our sensory information and resulting constructions of the world are integrated in the central nervous system. We can learn to see the shape of a pyramid and, without having touched one before, can identify the pyramid shape with our fingers through touch and manipulation even with our eyes closed.

REFLEXES

We are born with a few reflexes that are designed to help us with survival long enough for our strength, development, and experience to take over. These reflexes include breathing, sucking, swallowing, grasping, and keeping the body balanced in relation to the head position. While we are using these reflexes in relation to the environment, there is a tendency for the musculature involved to grow stronger, a tendency to repeat those things which are pleasurable, and eventually, a tendency to override the innate reflexes. New experiences tend to be repeated for their own sake. These repetitions lead to a system of organizing the environmental stimuli. Increasing new inputs and repetitions lead to reconstructions of older or inaccurate previous constructions. We often refer to this process as differentiation and generalization. As we experience different elements in our environment, we begin to note differences, and as this occurs we generalize about what elements we have differentiated. These things taste good, these things taste awful. Smooth things feel pleasant, prickly things feel bad. We are surprised when a prickly-looking leaf or material feels smooth. Throughout life we construct and reconstruct what we learn from the world and make use of it in the ways in which we behave and find contentment.

PROCESSES

Sensation and movement are processes and as such are very difficult to investigate because they don't stand still. They are always flowing in many directions and we suffer from the illusion that we can analyze them scientifically. The anatomical structures that make up sensation and movement are the parts of the process that can be looked at, touched and manipulated and put under a microscope, but only when they are not operative; only when they are no longer processes, but things. We are just beginning to develop instruments that can assess our mental processing while we are functioning, such as CAT Scans and MRI's.

We tend to assume that our sensory systems pick up images, sounds, models of the objects and events of the world just as they really are. We are usually unaware of raw stimuli because we have constructed our own worlds, providing a place and form of recognition for everything based on our previous experiences and constructions. Perception involves detection, comparison and recognition.

Visual stimulation is a pattern of excitation--light waves, particles--transmitted by the visual receptors to the visual receiving area at the back of the brain. Once we have selected what to focus on and what to omit through our capacity to discern figure/ground, very little of the possible range of stimuli is transmitted at all. In addition to the ways in which we have constructed the world, our needs and motivations are important in determining what we experience. A hungry person only looks for food, not warmth. A cold person looks for warmth--blankets, clothing, the thermostat--but not food. We select those things that are important to us, then we compare them and contrast them to previous experiences and constructs, and finally we construct a new world of our own, a world upon which to act.

INTEGRATION OF THE CENTRAL NERVOUS SYSTEM

The elements usually included in most models of the functioning central nervous system are input, integration, and output. But many models include an indirect feedback system, indicating the success of our response after it has taken place. More recent researchers also include a direct feedback loop of tactual and kinesthetic information indicating how we are moving as we are moving. This continuous monitoring gives us control while movements are in progress. When I am typing on my computer, I know I am making a "misteak" as I am making it through my kinesthetic and tactual feedback systems. I don't have to wait to read my "misteaks" later.

See diagram of the Integration Of The Central Nervous System on the following page.

INTEGRATION
OF THE
CENTRAL NERVOUS SYSTEM
DIAGRAM

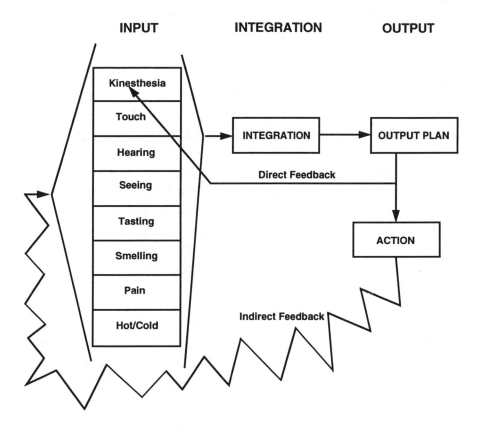

AUTOMATION

Several automatic actions can occur at one time. When I am driving to San Francisco, my right ankle is extended with my foot on the gas pedal, varying the pressure and relaxation as the speed needs to change, my eyes are watching the road ahead and behind, my left hand is on the steering wheel with varying degrees of rotation as the road varies, my right hand is holding a hamburger, bringing it to and from my mouth while my mouth opens and closes, tastes, chews, swallows, and starts all over again. At the same time, I am listening to the news on the radio and to my friend with varying changes in figure/ground as my attention wanes. I am making appropriate adjustments for driving in rain, snow, sleet, allowing for crazy drivers, deer and rocks, while computing the speed of the car, the curvature of the road, direction, wind, rate of progressive increase or decrease of speed, how fast to turn the wheel, etc., etc.

The miracle is that we can do all these things at once without any apparent strain. The incoming data is processed immediately and continuously while various movement programs are started by the higher levels of the central nervous system. The movements are carried out by numerous subroutines at various lower levels, especially the cerebellum. Unless something does not fit the projected outcome, these programs are kept at the subcortical levels. If circumstances change, varying amounts of conscious attention may be directed toward these occurrences. If all goes well and as predicted, the frontal lobe of the cerebral cortex is relatively free to pick and choose the focus of attention. We are consciously aware of paying attention only when something unusual happens.

Most of us have thousands of automatic subroutines that get us through most of our activities throughout the day without conscious attention. We therefore can think about all kinds of things, other than what we are actually doing, most of the time.

Some youngsters and adults have not developed or stored enough appropriate automatic patterns. They may have to focus their attention on which part of the body to move next, and how, instead of having the freedom to think about other things. With planning and practice, especially early in life, these automatized abilities can be developed and stored at various levels of the central nervous system.

COMPLEXITY

As we grow and interact with the environment, we must learn to develop more and more complex thinking functions rather than merely adding up quantitative learnings. As we continuously have more and more experiences and take in more and more information, we need to learn new ways to organize reality so that increased information becomes useful, not just massive. It is how we organize data that is important, not just the gathering of data.

In the beginning, we can only deal with small pieces of information at one time. As our information and experiences increase, we can learn to deal with each thing in relation to other things, each event in relation to other events. Soon we find that everything is interrelated with everything else and the world becomes one of relationships not single events in isolation.

One way that we make sense of our experiences is to make maps in our heads of the relationships around us, in much the same way that a map of California represents the interrelationships of the elements that make up the actual Sate of California. Think for a moment about how you can get from where you are now, to your car, to the grocery store, to where the milk is kept, and you are evoking one of your thousands of maps that are part of your universe. Writing involves the mapping out of various shapes called letters into sequences called words that make sentences that convey meaning. With practice, the actual act of writing is mostly automatic even though it involves mapping relationships. Hopefully, the conscious part of writing will be directed at the relationships of meaning that we are trying to convey, rather than the forming of letters and words. We have many other maps, like one for computing numbers, for speaking French, for taking a shower, and putting your socks on before reaching for your shoes.

Recent research of learning environments indicates that an enriched environment with many toys and activities produces laboratory animals that have significantly higher intelligence scores than do dull environments, with no toys or activities. These enriched environments develop better blood supplies, more transmitter fluids and more synaptic activity in the central nervous system of these animals than do empty environments. Research on humans indicates that we develop in similar ways.

The relationships between sensation, movement, thinking and feeling are the main determinants of what we are, who we are and what we can do. Through an understanding of these important relationships, as well as appropriate sensory/movement experiences, our self-awareness will have a direct bearing on our ability to live effectively and with confidence. We will be able to correct faulty subroutines that have not become properly automatic and learn to use conscious direction in initiating movements and actions that will lead to more efficient sensory data gathering and movement production.

Chapter 9

WHAT NEXT?

Now that you and your child have learned and improved in many abilities, it is time to reassess where you both are in relation to the initial goals you set for yourselves.

REASSESS

Check out your child's likes and dislikes in movement activities. Are these related to competence in specific areas. Does your child like swimming better than softball because she can't hit the ball or run in a straight line very well? Does she like to play catch or does she prefer running games like tag? In some instances you might want to go back to some of the activities in the appropriate chapter to strengthen weaknesses that you perceive. In other instances, it will be best to pursue those activities in which your child is already competent and ready to learn more. If she loves to run, you might check out local possibilities in track or soccer. If she like to play catch, maybe baseball, basketball or handball will fit nicely into her abilities and preferences. If she is highly tactual she might enjoy raising animals, whittling, or playing musical instruments. She might have several preferences and enjoy camping trips or planning swimming meets or homecoming parades. These main competency areas will probably be the activities that will last a lifetime.

DEVELOP STRENGTHS

Start your child thinking about something physical to pursue, whether it is a sport, such as swimming or gymnastics, an art form, such as drawing or graphics, a musical form of expression, such as piano or dance or anything that she enjoys, from hiking to rock collecting to the study of dinosaurs.

There are many many contributions a parent or teacher can make in any child's life. The more you both interact happily and constructively the more trust will be developed in both directions. Unfortunately, the main role that some parents and teachers play is that of "corrector". Whenever the child does something wrong, the corrector corrects. If that is all the parent or teacher does, it may build perfection, but it will also build fear, frustration, and low self-esteem.

Continue interacting with your child as educator and friend. If she chooses to play soccer, learn what you can about the game and practice with her in your backyard. If she chooses to be a sculptor, learn with her about the different processes she can use, different media, and alternative ways of learning about sculpture. If she chooses to play the cello, help her rent or buy a proper instrument, find a good teacher, and help her to seek out music for cello solos.

Find out what kinds of movement opportunities are available at the child's school as well as the local recreation center.

Choice of vacation places and events can play a part in providing opportunities for exposure to new interesting possibilities or to strengthening old beloved activities.

Tell your child the good things about her performance while encouraging her to reach a little farther, jump a little higher, run a little longer...if that is what she wants to do.

ONGOING ASSESSMENT

Assessment is ongoing. As the child continues to grow and gain skill and competence, her preferences will change. Often it will be important for the parent or teacher to continue to participate in the child's activities. At some point the child needs to learn to go on alone pursuing her goals in her own way without your influence.

Independence is essential to our growth into adulthood and it must be started early in our lives, not just when we reach the age of 21. Small efforts at independence, like small successes, lead to larger ones as we meet with challenges and opportunities.

You both have a wonderful world of opportunity to excel in the things you and she enjoy and love.

EMPOWER YOUR CHILD!

BIBLIOGRAPHY

1) Armstrong, Thomas. <u>Awakening Your Child's Natural Genius</u>. Jeremy P. Tarcher, 1991.

2) Baldwin, Rashima. <u>You Are Your Child's First Teacher</u>. Celestial Arts, 1989.

3) Bailey, Rebecca Anne and Elsie Carter Burton. <u>The Dynamic Self</u>. St. Louis, MO: CV Mosby, 1982.

4) Bossenmeyer, Linda. <u>Perceptualmotor Development Guide</u>. Byron, CA: Front Row Experience, 1988.

5) Brehm, Madeleine and Nancy T. Tindell. <u>Movement With A Purpose: Perceptual Motor Lesson Plans For Young Children</u>. West Nyack, NY: Parker Publishing, 1983.

6) Calvin, William H. <u>The Throwing Madonna: Essays On The Brain</u>. New York, NY: McGraw-Hill, 1983.

7) Capon, Jack. <u>Perceptual-Motor Lesson Plans, Level-1</u>. Byron, CA: Front Row Experience, 1975.

8) _____. <u>Perceptual-Motor Lesson Plans, Level-2</u>. Byron, CA: Front Row Experience, 1975.

9) _____. <u>Successful Movement Challenges</u>. Byron, CA: Front Row Experience, 1981.

10) Churchland, Patricia Smith. <u>Neurophilosophy: Toward A Unified Science Of Mind-Brain</u>. Cambridge, MA: MIT Press, 1986.

11) Cornell, Joseph. <u>Sharing The Joy Of Nature: Nature Activities</u>

For All Ages. Nevada City, CA: Dawn Publications, 1989.

12) Curtis, Sandra R. The Joy Of Movement In Early Childhood. New York, NY: Teachers College, Columbia University, 1982.

13) Cutting, James. Perception With An Eye For Movement. Cambridge, MA: MIT Press, 1986.

14) Cutright, Melitta. Growing Up Confident. New York, NY: Doubleday, 1992.

15) Daarst, Paul W. and George P. Armstrong. Outdoor Adventure Activities For School And Recreation Programs. Minneapolis, MN: Burgess, 1980.

16) Doman, Glenn. Teaching Your Baby Math. New York, NY: Simon And Schuster, 1979.

17) _____, Teaching Your Baby To Read. New York, NY: Doubleday, 1983.

18) Ellerbrook, Wallace C. "Hypotheses Toward A Unified Field Theory Of Human Behavior", ETC., June 1976.

19) Gallahue, David. Understanding Motor Development. Indianapolis, IN: Benchmark Press, 1989.

20) Gibson, Eleanor J. Principles Of Perceptual Learning And Development. Englewood Cliffs, NJ: Prentice Hall, 1969.

21) Gibson, James J. The Senses Considered As Perceptual Systems. Prospect Heights, IL: Waveland Press, 1966.

22) Grasselli, Rose N. and Priscilla A. Hegner. Playful Parenting. New York, NY: Perigee, 1981.

23) Hopper, Chris. The Sports Confident Child: A Parent's Guide To Helping Children. New York, NY: Pantheon Books, 1986.

24) Humphrey, James H. and Jay N. Humphrey. Help Your Child Learn The Three R's Through Active Play. Springfield, IL: Charles C. Thomas.

25) Jacobson, Edmund, Progressive Relaxation. Chicago, IL: University Of Chicago Press, 1938.

26) Kamii, Constance and Rheta De Vries. Physical Knowledge In Preschool Education: Implications Of Piaget's Theory. Englewood Cliffs, NJ: Prentice-Hall, 1978.

27) _____.Group Games In Early Education: Implications Of Piaget's Theory. Washington DC: National Association For The Education Of Young Children, 1980.

28) Kelley, Earl. Education For What Is Real. New York, NY: Harper & Row, 1947.

29) Kephart, Newell. The Slow Learner In The Classroom. Columbus, OH: Charles E. Merrill, 1971.

30) Kevington, Kenneth A. The Science Of Mind. Cambridge, MA: MIT Press, 1989.

31) Koestler, Arthur. The Ghost In The Machine. London, England: Arkana, 1989.

32) Leithwood, Kenneth A. "Motor, Cognitive And Affective Relationships Among Disadvantaged Preschool Children", The Research Quarterly, Vol. 42, No. 1, pp. 47-53, 1971.

33) Loye, David. The Sphinx And The Rainbow. Boulder, CO: Shambala, 1983.

34) Meyers, Russell, "The Proprioceptive Matrix Of Abstractions Called Mass, Energy, Space And Time", <u>ETC.</u>, December 1976, pp. 389-405.

35) Ontario Science Center. <u>Sportsworks: More than 50 Fun Activities That Explore The Science Of Sport</u>. Reading, MA: Addison-Wesley, 1989.

36) Orlick, Terry. <u>The Cooperative Sports And Games Book: Challenge Without Competition</u>. New York, NY: Pantheon, 1978.

37) Ornstein, Robert. <u>The Evolution Of Consciousness</u>. New York, NY: Prentice-Hall, 1991.

38) _____ and Paul Ehrlich. <u>New World/New Mind: Moving Toward Conscious Evolution</u>. New York, NY: Doubleday, 1989.

39) Piaget, Jean. <u>The Origins Of Intelligence in Children</u>. New York, NY: International Universities Press, 1952.

40) _____. <u>The Child's Conception Of Reality</u>. Totowa, NJ: Littlefield, Adams, 1972.

41) _____. <u>The Child And Reality</u>. New York, NY: Penguin, 1976.

41) Radler, D.H. and Newell C. Kephart. <u>Success Through Play: How To Prepare Your Child For School Achievement And Enjoy It</u>. New York, NY: Harper and Row, 1960.

42) Satir, Virginia. <u>Self Esteem</u>. Berkeley, CA: Celestial Arts, 1975.

43) Singer, Dorothy G. and Tracey A. Revenson. <u>How The Child Thinks: A Piaget Primer</u>. New American Library, 1978.

44) Van Witsen, Betty. <u>Perceptual Training Activities Handbook</u>. New York, NY: Teachers College Press, Columbia University, 1979.

45) Winnick, Joseph P. and French, Ronald W. <u>Piaget For Regular And Special Physical Educators And Recreators</u>. Brockport, NY: The Bookstore, 1975.

46) Zion, Leela C. and Betty Lou Raker. <u>The Physical Side Of Thinking</u>. Springfield, IL: Charles C. Thomas, 1986.

FREE PUBLISHER'S CATALOG!

Call toll-free or write for our free catalog of

INNOVATIVE CURRICULUM GUIDEBOOKS
AND
MATERIALS

for
Movement Education, Special Education,
and
Perceptual-Motor Development
(includes movement coordination equipment)

Call Toll-Free:
1-800-524-9091

or write:

FRONT ROW EXPERIENCE
540 Discovery Bay Blvd.
Byron, CA 94514-9454